Animal Senses

Phil Gates

CAMBRIDGE
UNIVERSITY PRESS

Cambridge Reading

General Editors
Richard Brown and Kate Ruttle

Consultant Editor
Jean Glasberg

Published by the Press Syndicate of the University of Cambridge
The Pitt Building, Trumpington Street, Cambridge CB2 1RP
40 West 20th Street, New York, NY 10011-4211, USA
10 Stamford Road, Oakleigh, Melbourne 3166, Australia

First published 1996

Animal Senses
Text © Phil Gates 1996
Illustrations © Rebecca Archer 1996 (title page, pages 2-3, 4-5, 6, 8-9, 10-11, 12, 14-15, 17, 18-19, 20, 23, 24); © Toni Hargreaves 1996 (pages 13 and 22)

Printed in Great Britain at the University Press, Cambridge

A catalogue record for this book is available from the British Library

ISBN 0 521 49934 8 paperback

Picture Research: Callie Kendall

Acknowledgements

We are grateful to the following for permission to reproduce photographs:

Front cover, Lawrence Watts; *back cover*, 13, 14, Frank Greenaway/Bruce Coleman Ltd; *title page*, 16*t*, Kim Taylor/Bruce Coleman Ltd; 4 (except 4*bl*), Graham Portlock ABIPP; 4*bl*, Tick Ahearn; 5 (owl), 18, 21, Gordon Langsbury/Bruce Coleman Ltd; 5 (dog), Leonard Lee Rue/Bruce Coleman Ltd; 5 (chameleon), 9, 17, Stephen Dalton/Natural History Photographic Agency; 5 (bat, spider), 7*l*, 8*t*, 10*t*, 15, 16*b*, Jane Burton/Bruce Coleman Ltd; 6, 7*r*, Hans Reinhard/Bruce Coleman Ltd; 7*b*, Lawrence Watts; 8*b*, Barrie Wilkins/J&B Photographers; 10*b*, Jeremy Grayson/Bruce Coleman Ltd; 11, N.G. Blake/Bruce Coleman Ltd; 12, Fritz Prenzel/Bruce Coleman Ltd; 16*l*, Phil Gates; 19, Konrad Wothe/Bruce Coleman Ltd; 20 (*main pic*), John Cox/Life File; 20 (*inset*), Roger Tidman/Natural History Photographic Agency; 22, John Shaw/Bruce Coleman Ltd.

Contents

Five senses

There are five senses which help people to find out about everything around them.

Touch

Sight

Taste

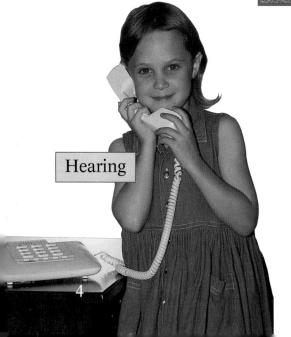

Hearing

Smell

Most animals have the same five senses.

Touch

Sight

Taste

Hearing

Smell

But some animals have
an extra sense, too.

Touch

Feeling with whiskers

Have you ever tried to touch a cat's whiskers? The cat will move its head away quickly because its whiskers are very sensitive.

A cat takes great care of its whiskers.

A cat's whiskers are about as wide as its body. It uses them to find out if a space is big enough for its body to get through.

This rabbit has long whiskers.

This Weddell seal touches the ice with its whiskers.

Lots of animals use their whiskers to help them to feel their way around.

Moles live in dark tunnels under the ground. They cannot see very well, so they feel their way along their tunnels with their whiskers.

Learning by touch

An octopus uses its tentacles to find out about the things around it. When the octopus sees something interesting, it touches it with its tentacles. The tentacles are covered with sensitive suckers.

A lion has very sensitive skin on its paws. This lion touches a porcupine with its paw to find out what the porcupine feels like.

Feeling game

- Ask a friend to put some small toys inside a large bag.
- Close your eyes and put your hands in the bag.
- Can you find out what the toys are just by touching them?

Feeling vibrations

We must seem like giants to small animals. When we walk about, small animals can feel the ground shaking because our footsteps make it vibrate. When small animals feel the vibrations, they try to hide.

Some small animals can run away. A snail cannot run, so it hides in its shell.

Beat the drum

- Put some rice, or some small beads, onto the skin of a drum.
- Bang your hand once on the drum. The drum skin vibrates.
- What happens to the rice?

9

A spider holds on to its web with its feet. When a fly lands on the web, the web vibrates. The spider can feel these vibrations with its feet.

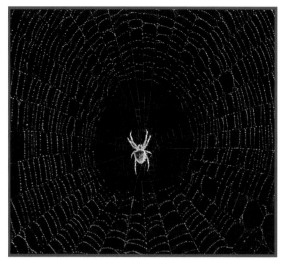

A pond skater
A pond skater is an insect that can walk on the surface of a pond. When another insect lands on the pond it makes ripples on the surface of the water. The pond skater feels these ripples under its feet and runs across the surface to catch and eat the insect.

Ripples

- Drop a small bead into a bowl of water.
- Can you see the ripples spreading across the surface of the water?

Hearing

Ears

Some animals have big ears which help them to hear very quiet sounds.

Big ears

- Make some large ears. You could use empty ice-cream tubs.

Hold one behind each ear. What happens when you wear your giant ears?

Horses can twist their ears around to listen to sounds that are coming from all directions. This helps them to listen out for danger.

Dogs can hear sounds that we cannot hear.

Some people use special dog whistles to call their dogs. The whistle makes a very high note that our ears cannot hear.

Bats' ears

Bats fly at night in the dark. They cannot see well, but they can hear very well. They use their hearing to stop themselves from crashing into things.

When a bat flies around, it makes squeaky sounds. The bat can hear the echo of these sounds, bouncing back from walls and trees.

If the bat hears the sounds bouncing back too quickly then it knows that it is about to crash into something, so it changes direction.

Echo game

If you throw a ball at a wall, the ball will bounce back to you. The closer you are to the wall, the quicker the ball will bounce back.

The echo of the bat's squeak works like the ball.

Bats eat insects. A bat uses its squeaky sounds to find insects that are flying in the air.

Sight

Eyes

Owls need to have very large eyes because they hunt at night. The light from the moon is not very bright, but an owl's large eyes can let in lots of moonlight.

The owl's eyes have very large pupils. Our eyes have pupils, too. The pupils look like black dots in the centre of our eyes, but they are really holes which let light in.

Try this

- Ask a friend to stand in a place where the light is bright. Look at your friend's eyes. Look carefully at the pupils.

- Now ask your friend to shut their eyes for 30 seconds.

- When they open their eyes, look at the pupils again. What do you see happening?

When it is dark, the pupils get bigger so that as much light as possible can get into the eyes.

When it is light, the pupils become smaller. This stops too much light from getting into the eyes and hurting them.

Cats' eyes

Cats can see very well in the dark because the pupils of their eyes grow very large and so let in lots of moonlight.

The insides of a cat's eyes are like mirrors. Light goes into their eyes and then it is reflected back again. At night, this makes it look as though the cat's eyes are shining.

We put rows of mirrors in the middle of dark country roads. These mirrors are called 'cat's eyes'. The light from car headlamps reflects back from the mirrors and so the mirrors shine. This helps drivers to see where the road is going.

Insects' eyes

An insect's eye is made up of lots of tiny eyes that are joined together.

The insect sees a picture that is made up of lots of coloured dots.

The eyes of a dragonfly cover most of its head, so it can look forwards, backwards and sideways to find its food.

Snails' eyes

Snails have eyes on the ends of stalks which grow longer when the snails come out of their shells.

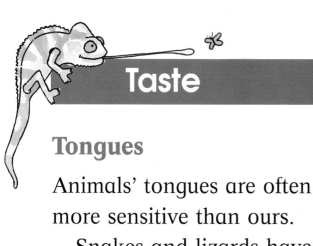

Taste

Tongues

Animals' tongues are often more sensitive than ours.

Snakes and lizards have forked tongues which they flick in and out all the time, tasting the air.

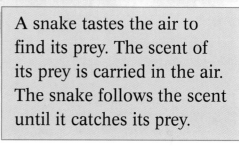

A snake tastes the air to find its prey. The scent of its prey is carried in the air. The snake follows the scent until it catches its prey.

A chameleon uses its long tongue to catch its food.

Smell

Noses

Dogs use their noses to find out about the world around them. They can find scents that we cannot smell at all.

A dog uses its nose to find out where other dogs have been.

A dog smells someone's hand to find out if it knows them.

Scent trails

Dogs can follow a trail of scent. They can remember one scent and sniff it out.

A dog can even use its nose to find a bone that it has buried under the ground.

Ants leave a trail of scent when they go to look for food. They can follow the trail of scent to find their way home again.

Secret senses

Finding the way home

Some animals have special, extra senses which people do not really understand.

If homing pigeons are taken hundreds of miles from their homes, they are always able to find their way home again. How do they know which way to fly?

A homing pigeon's home is called a loft.

Migration

At the end of summer, ospreys fly to Africa to find food and warmth for the winter. The journey that they make is called migration.

Young ospreys fly on their own to Africa when they are only a few months old. They have never flown to Africa before, so how do they find their way there?

The parent ospreys leave for Africa first. The young ospreys are not yet strong enough to make the journey and so they stay behind to eat more food.

When they are strong enough, the young ospreys fly on their own for thousands of miles.

A salmon's last journey

When a salmon nears the end of its life, it swims from the sea back up the river to the place where it hatched. There, the female salmon lays her eggs.

How does the salmon find its own river? Perhaps the river water has a scent that the salmon can remember and find.

When salmon swim up the river they have to swim against the water current. They often have to leap up waterfalls. The journey is long and tiring.

Young salmon hatch out of their eggs. When they are strong enough, they will swim down the river to live in the sea.

Glossary

echo   When a sound echoes, it bounces back from something so that you hear it again. If you shout in a tunnel, you can hear the *echo* of your voice bouncing back from the walls of the tunnel.

migration   Some animals and many birds make a long journey just before winter comes. They go to warmer countries where they can find food. In spring, they journey back again. This journeying from country to country is called *migration*.

prey   An animal's *prey* is another animal that it hunts to kill and eat.

pupils   The holes in the centre of our eyes are called *pupils*. They let light into our eyes.

ripples   *Ripples* are little waves which spread over the surface of water.

scent   An animal's smell is called its *scent*.

sense   Touch, hearing, sight, taste and smell are the *senses* which animals use to find out about everything around them.

surface   The *surface* is the outside or top part of something. The top of a table is a surface. Leaves often float on the surface of water.

vibration   When something vibrates it shakes very quickly. This shaking movement is called *vibration*. If you put your hand on a washing machine when it is working, you can feel the vibrations of the machine.

whiskers   Some animals have sensitive hairs on their faces which help them to feel things. These are called *whiskers*.

Index